"We must make them see
that we are the enemy ...
So let them turn the money
for defense in our direction
and either destroy us or
cure the conditions that
brought our people to this
point."

—Malcolm X

ISBN: 1-56584-032-1

LC: 92-61377

Published by the New Press, 1992
Originally published as Raw One-Shot #6, 1986

Printed in Hong Kong

THE NEW PRESS

PICTURES BY SUE COE

"CONCURRENT EVENTS" BY JUDITH MOORE

EDITED AND DESIGNED BY FRANÇOISE MOULY

RAW
ONE-SHOT

THE NEW PRESS • NEW YORK

Born Free
In the West
The Individual is best
To Hell with all the rest!

FREE WEST (West was framed!)

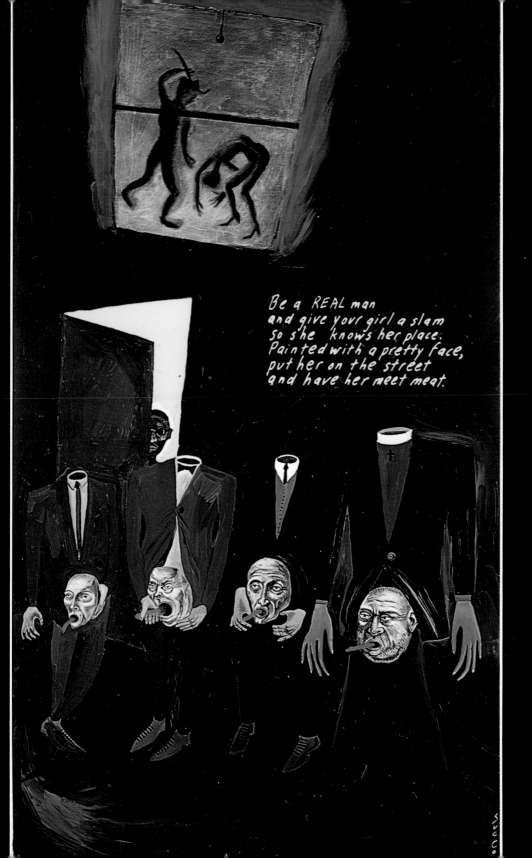

Be a REAL man
and give your girl a slam
so she knows her place.
Painted with a pretty face,
put her on the street
and have her meet meat.

The Right to Life,
  the Righteous laugh,
will help divide
    the Better Half.
Oh darling daughter,
  save from slaughter
those dear sperms
doomed to short terms.
And remember:
  All that is sacrosanct
  Must be banked.

So, "SNAP!" crackles Der Pope, that King of the Beasts
"I just put a ban on all progressive priests ...."
The shadow of the cross
runs on prophets.... not loss!

The video priests are gorged on feasts
of Fear, Guilt and Stupidity.
So pray to that holy Trinity.

Heroes:
Those who exploit best.

Losers:
Those who identify with the rest.

CONCURRENT EVENTS

1955

■ X, born Malcolm Little, became a Muslim during six-year incarceration for burglary. "I finished the eighth grade in Mason, Michigan. My high school was the black ghetto of Roxbury, Massachusetts. My college was in the streets of Harlem, and my master's was taken in prison."

■ In US golf is played by 3.8 million people on 5000 courses, the latter encompassing 1.5 million acres (2.5 persons per acre). Greater Harlem accommodates 542,000 people on 2,207 acres (245 persons per acre).

■ After his conversion X wrote, each day, to Elijah Muhammad, Messenger of Allah and leader since 1934 of the Nation of Islam. X, now, has been out of prison for 18 months. In June, 1954, Elijah Muhammad named X Minister of New York City's Temple Seven. Members are required to give up certain foods, liquor, drugs, dancing, movies, fornication and adultery. Nation women must obey husbands and dress modestly. Moral laws are policed by Fruit of Islam, Muslim men. Infractions bring suspension, or isolation, or, even expulsion. Separatists, the Nation eschews integration with the "blonde, blue-eyed devil," urges members to build economic power, and hopes, eventually, to found a separate Afro-American nation. The Nation is particularly successful among poor blacks in Northern cities and prisoners.

■ X understands the final degradation of self-hatred. Later he'll say: "We hated our head, we hated the shape of our nose—we wanted one of those long, *dog*-like noses, you know . . . It made us feel inferior. It made us feel inadequate. It made us feel helpless . . . " X invents black pride.

■ Popular songs: Bill Haley's "Rock Around the Clock" "The Yellow Rose of Texas," "Davy Crockett," "Sixteen Tons."

■ James Baldwin's *Notes of a Native Son* published.

January

1 US gives $216 million aid to South Vietnam.

12 US Secretary of State John Foster Dulles states "massive retaliation" policy, says US will retaliate "instantly by means and at places of our choosing."

31 60,000 black South Africans begin peaceful 13-day protest against government plan to move them to new town outside Johannesburg. Forced removal of blacks from homes begins on 9 February.

April

29 Civil war breaks out in Saigon as rebels opposed to US-backed Premier Ngo Dinh Diem lob mortar shells into Diem's palace.

May

12 In NYC Third Avenue El train ends service.

17 One year earlier, in Brown vs. Board of Education, the Supreme Court rules that segregation by color in public schools violates 14th

---

Amendment to the Constitution. At the time, President Eisenhower (Ike) told Supreme Court Justice Earl Warren, "All opponents of desegregation are concerned about is to see that their sweet little girls are not required to sit in schools alongside some big overgrown Negroes."

31 Supreme Court orders public schools integrated with "all deliberate speed."

August

28 14-year old Emmett Till, black, alleged to have "whistled at a white woman," lynched in Money, Mississippi.

September

Labor Day Three years ago Malcolm Little received his X from Chicago Temple Number Two. The X is substituted for the slave name given to slaves by plantation owners.

1 Till's body fished out of Tallahatchie River. All-white jury will acquit two white men accused of Till's murder.

30 James Dean crashes Porsche.

November

9 South Africa quits UN over apartheid.

December

1 Rosa Parks refuses to give her bus seat to Montgomery, Alabama, white man. Parks arrested. Eldridge Cleaver writes, "Somewhere in the universe a gear in the machinery shifted." 5 - Montgomery bus boycott begins. Martin Luther King, Jr., saying, "There comes a time when people get tired," accepts presidency of boycott organization.

1956

■ Elijah Muhammad authorizes Temple 7 to buy X a new Chevy.

■ In Atlanta, police rule that teenagers cannot dance to Rock & Roll in public without parental consent.

■ 20,000 TV sets bought daily. 500 stations in operation. Americans now spend more time watching TV than they spend working for pay.

January

11 Dulles issues Cold War policy statement. "We are in a contest in the field of economic development of underdeveloped countries which is bitterly competitive. Defeat in this contest could be as disastrous as defeat in an armaments race."

30 King's home bombed.

THERE IS NO GOD BUT ALLAH

February

1 South Africa orders USSR consulates closed, charging USSR spreads Communist propaganda among black and Indian population.

3 Autherine Lucy admitted to University of Alabama.

7 Lucy suspended after 'Bama students riot.

29 Lucy expelled — "Her presence threatens public order."

March

12 101 Southern congressmen call for massive resistance to Supreme Court desegregation rulings.

April

18 Grace Kelly marries Monaco's Prince Rainier.

May

■ "Fishing" for converts, opening new temples, X has put 30,000 miles on Chevy.

30 Bus boycott begins in Tallahassee, Florida.

June

5 Federal court rules racial segregation on Montgomery buses violates Constitution.

July

■ Ringling Brothers and Barnum and Bailey Circus performs last show under canvas tent.

August

30 White mob prevents enrollment of black students at Mansfield, Texas, high school.

September

2 Tennessee National Guard quells Clinton, Tennessee mobs demonstrating against school integration.

25 First transatlantic telephone cable goes into operation.

November

6 Ike and Nixon defeat Adlai Stevenson by landslide vote.

13 Supreme Court upholds lower court decision banning segregation on Montgomery city busses.

December

2 Fidel Castro and 82 Cuban exiles land in Cuba, initiating guerrilla campaign against President Batista.

21 Montgomery buses integrated.

Christmas Day Home of Birmingham, Alabama protest leader destroyed by dynamite.

26 Birmingham blacks begin mass defiance of Jim Crow bus laws.

1957

■ X organizes Los Angeles Temple, founds newspaper, *Mr. Muhammad Speaks.*

■ Elijah M sends X on three-week trip to Africa.

■ Jack Kerouac's *On the Road* published. In interview Beat poet Gregory Corso says: "Fried shoes. Like it means nothing. Don't shoot the warthog."

January

4 *Collier's* magazine and 85-year-old *Woman's Home Companion* fold.

19 Jerry Lewis's first TV special since split with Dean Martin.

March

6 British colony, the Gold Coast, becomes independent of British Commonwealth. Takes name of ancient African empire, "Ghana." 50 nations' dignitaries are welcomed to celebration by Premier Kwame Nkrumah.

24 "The Black Star Rises," CBS documentary on Vice President Richard Nixon's trip to Africa.

April

29 After internecine struggle, Congress approves emasculated Civil Rights Bill. Designed to protect black voting rights, by 1959 this legislation has not added one Southern black to voters' rolls.

May

2 Sen. Joseph McCarthy (R, Wisc) dies, mostly ignored.

4 & 11 "Rock 'n' Roll Show," first prime-time network special devoted to rock, hosted by Alan Freed, with Sal Mineo, the Clovers, Screamin' Jay Hawkins, and the Del-Vikings.

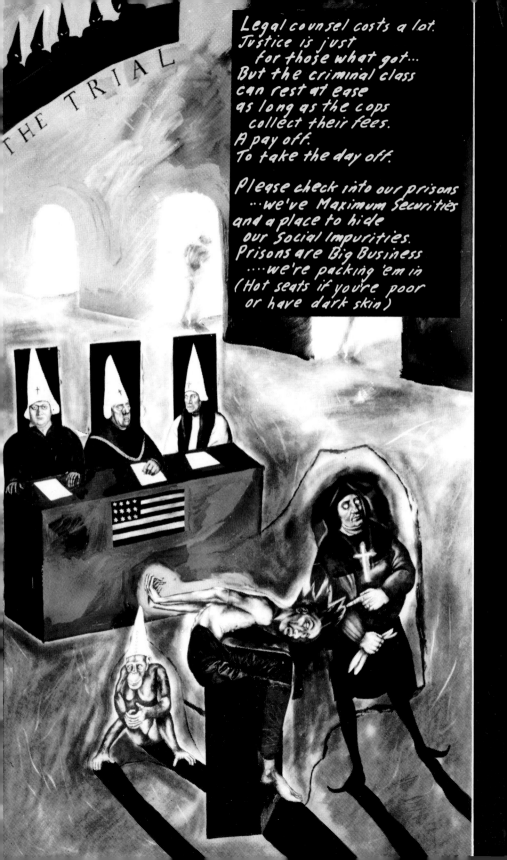

May

19 "The Rebels of Sierra Maestra - Cuba's Jungle Fighters," CBS news documentary on Cuban guerrillas, with an interview with Castro.

23 Florida Governor refuses to extradite Jewish Mr and Mrs Melvin B. Ellis on charge of kidnaping foster daughter Hildy, 6. They fled Massachusetts when courts ruled to separate them from their daughter because Hildy's natural mother was Catholic.

August

5 American Bandstand, hosted by 26-year-old Dick Clark, goes on network TV.

29 Congress passes first civil rights act in 82 years, establishes civil rights commission.

September

4 Arkansas National Guard bars nine black students from entering all-white Little Rock high school.

9 Nashville school with enrollment of 1 black and 388 whites destroyed by dynamite.

22 In Haiti Francois Duvalier, "Papa Doc," a favorite of military junta, made president.

25 Ike sends 1000 paratroopers to Little Rock to permit nine black students to attend the previously all-white high school.

26 Order to alert regular army units for riot duty in Southern cities canceled by Army Secretary.

October

4 USSR orbits Sputnik I, first earth satellite.

10 Ghana's Finance Minister refused service in Delaware restaurant. Ike apologizes.

November

3 USSR orbits Sputnik II, carrying an Eskimo dog.

27 Federal troops leave Little Rock.

1958

■ Approximately 50 million strips of polyethylene tubing formed into circles will be sold during the year. This is the year of the Hula Hoop®.

■ "Cha Cha" new dance craze.

January

13 Petition signed by 9000 scientists from 43 countries urging immediate end to nuclear testing presented to UN.

April

4 Police at Harlem's Precinct 28 receive call about fight between two black men at corner of 125th St. and 7th Ave. Spectators have gathered.

Police rush the crowd, among whom is onlooker Johnson Hinton (aka Johnson X), a Muslim. Police and Hinton "exchange words." Hinton, head split open, is knocked to the concrete, then taken to 28th Precinct Station. An hour later, 500-1000 Muslims surround the station. When X arrives at the station, he demands that Hinton, sprawled on cell floor in a pool of blood, be hospitalized at once *and* that the police acknowledge that Hinton was not at fault. This accomplished, X, disperses crowd. "No man," says precinct captain, "should have this much power over that many people. We cannot control this town if one man can wield that kind of power."

May

13 Nixon, on seven-nation Latin American goodwill tour, stoned by Caracas, Venezuela crowd.

August

■ State Department refuses again to recognize Mao's China, reasoning that "Communism's rule in China is not permanent."

9 Michael Jackson born.

27 USSR launches Sputnik III, carrying two dogs.

October

16 Cheating scandal erupts: last showing of NBC TV's two-season winner, quiz show Twenty-One.

1959

■ 1959 marks 30th anniversary of X's father's murder by Klan-like group in Lansing, Michigan.

■ Motown Records established.

January

1 Cuba's Batista flees. On February 15, Fidel Castro becomes Premier of Cuba; expropriates US-owned sugar mills.

February

■ South African college sets world record and start fad by cramming twenty-five people into a phone booth.

April

15 Castro begins private 11-day goodwill tour of eastern US, stays at Harlem's Hotel Theresa.

July

10 Mike Wallace and Louis Lomax produce "The Hate That Hate Produced," TV program on Nation of Islam. Membership, under 30,000, doubles within weeks.

17 Billie Holiday, 44, dies.

September

5-27 Khrushchev visits US, is refused permission to see Disneyland.

6 97 pound catfish reeled in in South Dakota.

December

11 Last Civil War soldier, aged 117, dies.

1960

■ US population: 179.3 million; black population 18.8 million. Percentage of families whose yearly income is:
below $ 3,000: . . . . Black 44%
below $ 5,000: . . . . Black = 68%
White = 36%
above $ 7,000: . . . . Black = 17%
White = 41%
above $10,000: . . . Black = 6%
White = 18%

■ 44% of black people live in substandard housing; 77% of urban blacks are confined to ghetto areas.

■ NAACP membership decline begins.

■ Popular songs: "Itsy Bitsy Teenie Yellow Polka Dot Bikini," "Let's Do the Twist," "Never on Sunday."

Heroes: Those who exploit best.
Losers: Those who identify with the rest.

The fetid stench
of capital
lingers where
the wealthy dwell.
It's called
oppression,
what a filthy smell.

DOG CATCHER

DOG FOOD INC
DOG FOOD INC

January

31 "The Fabulous Fifties:" CBS-TV retrospective hosted by Henry Fonda.

February

1 Sit-in movement born: four black students sit in at segregated North Carolina dime store counter. By year's end 50,000 people sit-in in over 100 cities, 3600 jailed.

17 Ike authorizes CIA training of Cuban exiles to invade Cuba.

May

1 US U-2 spy plane shot down over Soviet Union. Khrushchev refuses, then, to attend Paris Peace conference scheduled for May 16 unless Ike apologizes for US spying.

9 First oral contraceptive for women approved by FDA.

16 Paris Peace Conference canceled.

June

30 Zaire proclaims independence. During Sixties more than 30 African nations gain independence.

July

6 Ike orders 95% cut in Cuban sugar imports.

14 Ike reminds USSR of US's 1823 Monroe Doctrine prohibiting establishment in Western Hemisphere of "any despotic political system."

August

7 Black and white students stage kneel-in's in Atlanta churches.

September

26 First of four hour-long TV debates between presidential candidates John F. Kennedy (JFK) and Nixon.

October

12 Khrushchev, attending UN General Assembly's 15th session, pounds his shoe on table as he engages in argument with the Phillipine's delegate.

19 King arrested in Atlanta sit-in, ordered to serve 4 months in state prison for violating probated traffic sentence.

27 King released on bond.

November

8 JFK defeats Nixon by less than 100,000 votes.

1961

■ Nation of Islam flourishes, membership rises to 100,000, number of Muslim-owned businesses increases. Detroit and Chicago Universities of Islam offer high school diplomas. Muhammad, 65 now and increasingly debilitated by asthma. Nation buys home for him in Phoenix, Arizona. X, still deeply and entirely devoted to Muhammad, visits the Nation's leader — "this lamb of a man" — almost monthly.

■ Eric Lincoln's dissertation becomes first book about Nation, *The Black Muslims in America*, and coins name "Black Muslims." Book brings increasing publicity to Nation.

■ Popular songs: "Love Makes the World Go Round," "Moon River," "Exodus."

January

3 US severs diplomatic relations with Cuba.

11 Two black students enroll at University of Georgia. Riot ensues.

17 Patrice Lumumba, ousted Congo premier, assassinated.

17 In last speech to nation as president Ike warns of "military-industrial complex."

22 "The Red and the Black," ABC documentary on Soviet influence in Africa.

25 JFK's first press conference as president; first live telecast of Presidential news conference.

February

7 Jane Fonda makes first dramatic appearance on US TV.

March

1 JFK establishes Peace Corps.

13 JFK proposes Alliance for Progress, ten year program to help Latin America raise living standards.

April

17 1400 CIA trained and funded Cuban exiles land in Bay of Pigs, attempt to overthrow Castro. Attempt fails.

18 "90 Miles to Communism," ABC documentary on Cuba.

May

4 13 Freedom Riders begin bus trip through South.

5 Alan Shephard becomes first American to make sub-orbital space flight. Largest daytime TV audience in history watches him take his 15 minute ride into space.

14 Freedom Riders' bus bombed and burned in Alabama.

20 Mob attacks freedom riders in Montgomery. Governor declares martial law, calls out National Guard.

24 Freedom Riders arrive in Jackson, Mississippi, where Governor Ross Barnett has declared that "the Negro is different because God made him different to punish him."

31 South Africa declares independence.

August

17-18 East Germany erects Berlin Wall.

October

15 X on "Open Mind" NBC- television program. "There is a new so-called Negro in America," says X. "Not only is he impatient. Not only is he dissatisfied, not only is he disillusioned, but he's getting very angry."

November

14 JFK announces decision to increase US advisers in Vietnam from 1000 to 16,000 over next two years.

29 White mob attacks Freedom Riders at McComb, Mississippi, bus station.

December

12 700 demonstrators, including King, arrested in Albany, Georgia, in mass marches protesting segregation.

15 Tear gas and dogs used by Baton Rouge, Louisiana, police to stop demonstration by 1500 blacks.

15 Adolf Eichmann, accused of major role in Nazi murder of 6 million Jews, sentenced by a Jerusalem court to be hanged.

22 First US soldier in Vietnam killed by Viet Cong.

1962

■ Total world population: 3.1 billion; adult world adult population: 1.6 billion. 44% of adult population illiterate.

■ By the fall, the Twist is giving way to the Hully Gully, the Mashed Potato, the Majestic Slop, the Wobble, the Monkey (make like you're climbing a tree), the Philly Dog, the Watusi and the Chicken Back.

January

16 NYC Board of Education accused of using racial quotas in city's schools.

February

Valentine's Day JFK states that US troops in Vietnam will fire to protect themselves if fired upon, but are "not combat troops in the generally understood sense of the word."

■ "A Tour of the White House with Mrs. John F. Kennedy" on prime-time. "Jackie glasses" (wraparound sunglasses) are the craze of the year.

20 John Glenn becomes first American to orbit earth.

April

■ In LA police attack Muslims outside Islam temple. One Muslim dies, another paralyzed for life, five severely wounded. Elijah Muhammad stops X from seeking revenge.

20 New Orleans segregationists offer blacks free one-way tickets to Northern cities.

Stocks and shares, sharks and fishes,
All those yummy money dishes
dance in the Oceans of Finance.
The Money Market makes a watery grave
So float alone, you poor wage slaves,
working stiffs smashed by the banks of the sea.

The Money Temple

Profit, profit or run at a loss.
The tides of fortune know who's boss.
In the underwater world
    called Wall Street
Sharks cruise daily
    through a sea of meat.
When times are good they merger.
When times are bad they murder.

Heroes: Those who exploit best.
Losers: Those who identify with the rest.

Television, radio, tapes, CD's
Satellites beam across the seas
A chorus of vultures
croon the songs of our culture.
Sexism and Racism.... the lyrics that pay.
Oh, to hum the tunes of today.

Behind the newsman's smile gleams the shark's tooth,
Gas foams from his lips and passes for truth.
The Screech of Freedom is on the air,
broadcasting abroad with intent to ensnare.
When the master cracks his whip
the Networks dare not make a slip.

May

28 NAACP files suit alleging *de facto* segregation in Rochester, New York, schools.

31 Eichmann hanged.

June

3 121 Atlantans die in plane crash in Paris. X, in LA at inquest in death of LA Muslim, says, '' I would like to announce a very beautiful thing that happened . . . He really answered our prayers in France. He dropped an airplane out of the sky with over 120 white people on it because the Muslims believe in an eye for an eye and a tooth for a tooth.'' Later, on a talk show, when the emcee calls X's joy over the plane crash obscene, X says, ''Just as Americans thanked God when she dropped the bomb on Hiroshima that wiped out 100,000 Japanese, I think that we are well within our rights to thank God when he steps in.''

14 First victim of Boston Strangler found.

August

15 Between this date and September 25, 8 black churches burned in Georgia.

September

13 Mississippi Governor Ross Barnett defies US government, says he will not permit black student James Meredith to enter University of Mississippi (Ol' Miss). Says Barnett, ''There is no case in history where the Caucasian race has survived social integration.''

30 In Oxford, Mississippi, town and gown riot on Ol' Miss campus. Two killed, hundreds wounded.

October

1 3,000 US soldiers and National Guardsmen put down riots, Meredith enters Ol' Miss.

22 JFK announces: USSR has installed missiles in Cuba.

24 US blockades Cuba.

November

2 USSR will dismantle Cuban missile sites.

20 US lifts Cuban blockade.

■ In late 1962, rumors of Muhammad's immorality with women spread through Chicago's Temple Two.

1963

■ ''Beverly Hillbillies'' becomes US's most popular TV show.

■ Popular songs: ''Those Lazy, Hazy, Crazy Days of Summer,'' ''Call Me Irresponsible.''

■ Louisiana Citizens Council chapter offers $10,000 reward for X's death.

■ Muhammad makes X Nation of Islam's first National Minister.

■ Chubby Checker's smash hit ''Limbo Rock'' renews interest in the Limbo, originally a sacred funeral rite in the West Indies, now a party rouser.

January

■ 100 years ago Abraham Lincoln signed Emancipation Proclamation.

1 Philadelphia's traditional Mummers parade features blackface marchers for the last time.

2 30 US soldiers killed when five US helicopters are shot down in Vietnam's Mekong Delta.

February

19 USSR withdraws troops from Cuba.

March

1 Emancipation Centennial protests begin with voter registration campaign in Greenwood, Mississippi.

18 US Supreme Court orders that all criminal defendants must have counsel and that illegally acquired evidence is not admissible in state or federal courts.

April

2 King opens major civil rights campaign in Birmingham.

2 X flies to Phoenix, confronts Muhammad with rumors of latter's adulterous behavior with secretaries. Muhammad and his sons will accuse X of spreading these rumors.

May

■ Alex (*Roots*) Haley's *Playboy* interview with X hits newsstands.

■ At Yale, students riot to the cry of ''We want sex.'' Seventeen jailed, one injured by police.

2-7 In Birmingham police set dogs and high-pressure firehoses on demonstrators. 2500 arrested, including many children.

9 Vietnam's ''strategic hamlet'' program, resettling villagers in barbed wire compounds, begins.

11 JFK assigns federal troops to bases near Birmingham.

31 ''Angry Spokesman Malcolm X Tells Off Whites,'' *Life* magazine article.

June

10 South Vietnamese Buddhist priest burns himself to death in protest of persecution by government.

11 Two black students under National Guard escort, enroll at 'Bama despite Governor George Wallace's pledge to block the school house door.

12 Medgar Evers, NAACP Mississippi field secretary, assassinated.

12-13 Civil rights groups demonstrate at Harlem construction sites, protesting discrimination in building trades unions. Demonstrations, dramatizing anger over housing, school, and job discrimination continue throughout summer in Northeast cities.

17 Supreme Court rules recitation of Lord's Prayer or Bible verses in public schools unconstitutional.

18 3000 black Boston students protest school segregation.

July

■ *New York Times* reports X as second most sought after speaker at colleges and universities. Only presidential candidate Barry Goldwater is more popular.

3 Reports of Muhammad's relationship with secretaries reach newspapers.

Third World Nations?
Places for vacations.
White man mixes cops and bones
into sun-safe Coppertones.

U.S. military successfully bombs a mental hospital in Grenada

August

5 Nuclear Test Ban Treaty signed by US, Britain, USSR.

27 W.E.B. Du Bois, 95, dies in Ghana.

28 200,000, including X, who calls event the "Farce on Washington," attend March on Washington. X says, "Those 'integration'-mad Negroes ran over each other trying to find out where to sign up." King orates: "I have a dream that this nation will rise up and live out the true meaning of its creed." Says X, "And the black masses in America were — and still are — having a nightmare."

September

15 Birmingham church bombing kills four black girls, injures 20.

October

22 225,000 students boycott Chicago schools protesting *de facto* segregation.

25 "The World's Girls," ABC documentary looks at feminism, with Simone de Beauvoir, Simone Signoret, Betty Friedan.

November

1 With US complicity South Vietnam's president Diem assassinated.

22 CBS's Walter Cronkite interrupts soap opera, "As the World Turns," to tell nation that JFK has been seriously wounded in Dallas. JFK dead on arrival at Parklane Memorial Hospital. Lyndon Baines Johnson (LBJ) becomes 36th President.

22 Muhammad orders Muslim ministers: make no remarks about assassination.

23 X, asked about JFK's assassination, comments: "It's a case of the chickens coming home to roost."

24 Jack Ruby shoots Lee Harvey Oswald, alleged JFK assassin.

24 X silenced by Muhammad for 90 days.

December

■ At year's end US troops in South Vietnam total 15,000. More than $500 million in aid given to South Vietnam.

1964

■ *Jet* magazine reports that during presidential campaign Senator Goldwater told this joke:" A white man, a Negro, and a Jew were each given one wish. The white man asked for securities; the Negro asked for a lot of money; the Jew asked for some imitation jewelry 'and that colored boy's address'."

■ Popular songs: "Hello, Dolly!," "I Want to Hold Your Hand."

January

4 13th and last victim of Boston Strangler found dead in Beacon Hill

15 First discotheque "*Whiskey a Go-Go*" opens on Sunset strip in LA.

23 24th Amendment to Constitution eliminates poll tax requirements in federal elections.

February

3 464,000 black and Puerto Rican students boycott NYC public schools.

9 Beatles appear for first time on Ed Sullivan show, sing "All My Loving."

20-24 X and family invited to Cassius Clay's training camp.

25 Clay, soon to become Muhammad Ali, defeats Sonny (The Bear) Liston for world heavyweight boxing championship. X attends fight.

March

4 X resigns from Nation of Islam, organizes Muslim Mosque, Inc., plans trip to Mecca.

16 LBJ submits "War on Poverty" program to Congress.

April

19 X makes *hajj* (pilgrimage) to Mecca.

20 86% of black students participate in Cleveland, Ohio, school boycott.

May

21 X returns to NYC, having visited Egypt, Lebanon, Saudi Arabia, Liberia, Dakar, Nigeria, Ghana, Morocco and Algeria.

29 FBI visits X, asks X to give names of Nation of Islam members. X refuses.

June

16 In Queens' courtroom, white judge declares Nation of Islam rightful owner of X's Long Island home.

22 Three civil rights workers reported missing in Mississippi.

28 X founds Organization for Afro-American Unity (OAAU). X asserts that the OAAU is being formed to "bring about the complete independence of people of African descent in the Western Hemisphere."

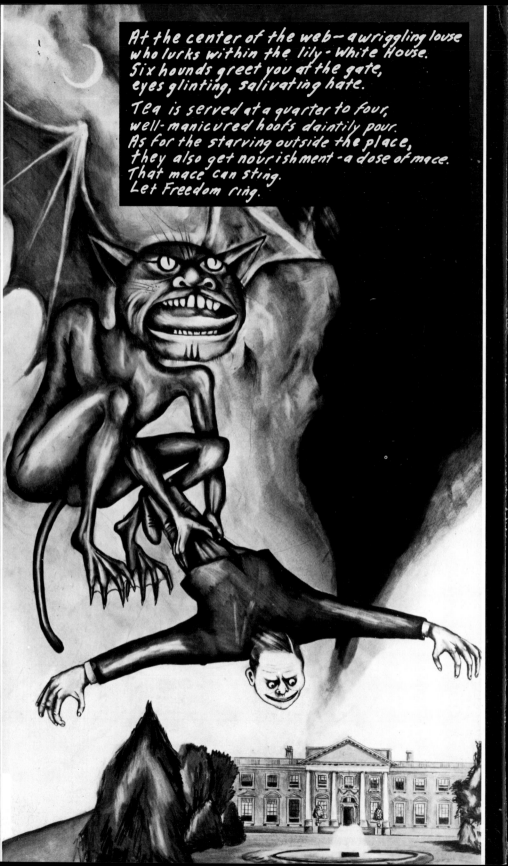

At the center of the web — a wriggling louse
who lurks within the lily - White House.
Six hounds greet you at the gate,
eyes glinting, salivating hate.

Tea is served at a quarter to four,
well-manicured hoofs daintily pour.
As for the starving outside the place,
they also get nourishment - a dose of mace.
That mace can sting.
Let Freedom ring.

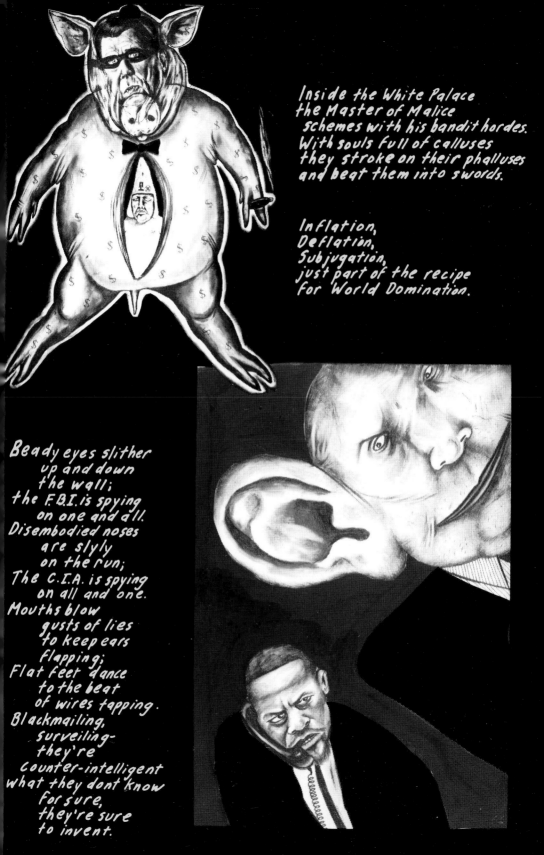

Inside the White Palace
the Master of Malice
    schemes with his bandit hordes.
With souls full of calluses
    they stroke on their phalluses
and beat them into swords.

Inflation,
Deflation,
Subjugation,
    just part of the recipe
for World Domination.

Beady eyes slither
    up and down
    the wall;
the F.B.I. is spying
    on one and all.
Disembodied noses
    are slyly
    on the run;
The C.I.A. is spying
    on all and one.
Mouths blow
    gusts of lies
    to keep ears
    flapping;
Flat feet dance
    to the beat
    of wires tapping.
Blackmailing,
    surveiling-
    they're
Counter-intelligent
what they don't know
    for sure,
    they're sure
    to invent.

WITCH HUNT

MALCOLM X

J. Edgar Hoover
was a shaker and a mover.
"Get King," he said.
King's now dead.

"We declare our right on
this earth to be a man, to be
a human being, to be
respected as a human being,
to be given the rights of a
human being, in this society,
on this earth, which we
intend to bring into
existence by any means
necessary."

—*Malcolm X*

Are these pictures all too dark for you?
Too much black? Too much blue?
Too much squalor? Too much crime
in this landscape of our time?
Then open your eyes,
X out their lies,
and work with your minds,
your hearts, your sinews
for a better world
.. Evolution continues
toward Freedom
by any means necessary.

BY ANY MEANS NECESSARY!

POLICE STATE   I saw this on Nov 2, 1985. SC

■ By year's end US forces in Vietnam number 184,300.

■ $30 million worth of skateboards sold at prices ranging from $1.98 to $50.

■ Go-go girls wearing mini-skirts and go-go boots fill the new discotheques.

January

4 LBJ in State of Union message describes Great Society goals: federal support of education, health, arts, urban renewal, water pollution.

■ Early in this month X speaks at SNCC meeting in Selma.

February

1 700 demonstrators, including King, arrested in Selma voter registration drive.

6 Viet Cong attack US base at Pleiku, killing 8 Americans, wounding 126.

7 LBJ orders continuous bombing of North Vietnam below 20th parallel.

9 X, invited to speak at Congress of African Students in Paris, is barred from entering France.

10 Viet Cong blow up US barracks at Quinhon, kill 23 US soldiers. 160 US and South Vietnamese planes bomb North Vietnam.

13-14 X's home firebombed. Betty X, pregnant, and four children, are disturbed.

15 James X, Minister of NYC's Temple 7, tells reporters X fire-bombed his own house to get publicity.

15 At morning meeting in Detroit X argues that ''colonialism or imperialism, as the slave system of the West is called,'' forms an ''international power structure''... ''used to suppress the masses of dark-skinned people all over the world and exploit them of their natural resources.''

''1965 will be the longest and hottest and bloddiest year of them all. It has to be, not because you want it to be, or I want it to be, or we want it to be, but because the conditions that created these explosions in 1963 are still here.''

15 Back in NYC, at Audubon Ballroom meeting, X says, ''My house was bombed by the Muslims!''

15 Nat King Cole dies.

19 Speaking of days with Nation, X tells friend about ''old Temple 7 days.'' ''That was a bad scene, brother. The sickness and madness of those days — I'm glad to be free of those days — I'm glad to be free of it. It's a time for martyrs now. And if I'm to be one, it will be in the cause of brotherhood. That's the only thing that can save this country. I've learned it the hard way — but I've learned it.''

20 X telephones Haley, says, ''I'm not at all sure it's the Muslims. I know what they can do, and what they can't, and they can't do some of the stuff recently going on... I think I'm going to quit saying it's the Muslims.''

21 In anteroom of Audubon Ballroom where X is scheduled to speak to OAAU meeting, X says 'I don't feel right about this meeting, I feel I should not be here. Something is wrong, brothers.' 2:30 p.m., X is introduced: ''I present a man who would give his life for you.'' ''As-Salaam Alaikum,'' says X, greeting audience, which replies, ''Wa-Alaikum Salaam.'' Shots ring out. X, 39, assassinated.

July

■ Whamo-O introduces Super Ball. 7 million will be sold at 98¢ a piece by Christmas.

August

11-16 Riots by blacks living in the Watts area of Los Angeles result in damages estimated at $200 million and death of 35.

■

June

29 Omnibus civil rights bill passed, banning discrimination in voting, jobs, public accommodations.

July

■ X, hoping to acquire Organization for African Unity (OAU) support for OAAU, leaves for 18-week trip to Africa. CIA follows him.

2 LBJ signs Civil Rights Act.

18-22 Harlem race riot spreads to Brooklyn's Bedford-Stuyvesant section.

25 Race riot, Rochester, NY.

August

2 Race riot, Jersey City, NJ.

4 Civil rights workers found buried. 21 white men, including several police officers, arrested. In 1967 seven of these men will be found guilty of conspiracy in the slayings.

7 Tonkin Resolution passed.

11-12 Race riot, Paterson, NJ.

12-13 Race riot, Elizabeth, NJ.

15-16 Race riot, Dixmoor, Chicago suburb.

20 LBJ signs Economic Opportunity Act.

28-30 Race riot, Philadelphia.

September

13 Khrushchev removed from power in USSR.

27 Warren Commission Report on JFK assassination released, finding no evidence of conspiracy.

November

3 LBJ wins landslide victory over Goldwater.

23 Latin ceases to be official language of Roman Catholic liturgy.

24 X returns to NYC from five-month African journey.

December

■ Sam Cooke killed.

4 Minister Louis X of Boston (aka Louis Farrakhan) issues death warrant on Malcolm when he publishes in *Muhammad Speaks*: ''TO FOLLOW MALCOLM IS TO BE DOOMED''. 'The die is set, and Malcolm will not escape.' ... ''such a man as Malcolm is worthy of death''.

10 King awarded Nobel Peace Prize.

16 X speaks at The Harvard Law School Forum: ''I believe in the brotherhood of all men, but I don't believe in wasting brotherhood on anyone who doesn't want to practice it with me.''

31 X speaks to 37 students visiting NYC from Mississippi, tells students things are no better for black man in North than in South.

At the Audubon ballroom a bird soared too high
and was shot down

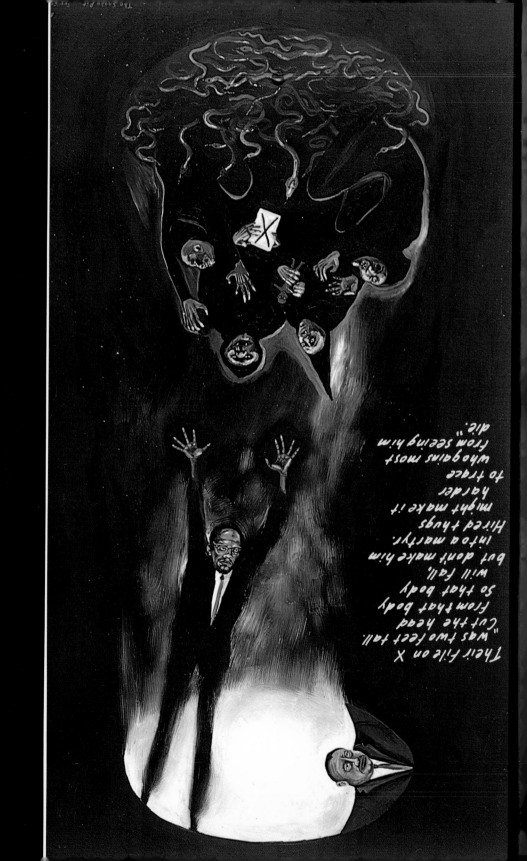

"Their file on X
was two feet tall.
Cut the head
from that body
so that body
will fall,
but dont make him
into a martyr.
Hired thugs
might make it
harder
to trace
who gains most
from seeing him
die."